1

Let me introduce myself.

My name is Glen Carloss, I'm 34 years old and I have been tattooing now for almost 9 years.

You are probably wondering why I wrote this short book and its simple....

I want to start by just saying that by no means am I a psychologist or mental health expert.
I am just a normal guy who struggles with his thoughts daily and I've come up with a simple technique for putting irrational thoughts out of my head.

Every day I go to work and throughout my day, my mind wanders.
Off I drift into a daydream about anything and everything......

Not a problem, if the thoughts I have are always nice, but... unfortunately for me and millions of us out there, we tend to focus on the negative thoughts instead of the positive ones!

If, like me, you have a vivid imagination and an overactive brain, then this can cause you daily issues. Anxiety, overanalysing, depression, eating disorders, just to name a few...

The trouble I have also is that because I have such an overactive imagination, I've found that most self-help books out there today, are either too long, too boring or just too complicated to keep me reading until the end.

Boring book

So, I have written a short book (with pictures!) to help all of us overthinkers, over analysers and worriers out there, who just need a quick fix and a simple technique to settle our thoughts and if you are anything like me, that's a lot of thoughts that need settling!

You're probably wondering at this point, who or what is the spiteful raisin... so let me explain....

The spiteful raisin is an angry spiteful little guy that can disguise himself into any way he sees fit;
Anxiety, irrational thoughts, paranoia, sad thoughts, silly worries, panic attacks, self-harm, alcohol/drug abuse etc.
He has one job and one job only and that is to ruin your day.

One of the most important things to remember about the spiteful raisin is
just how good he is at disguising himself!

Fold this page over, as you will want to remember that.

It's because of this, that the spiteful raisin is cleverer than we think.

Let me give you an example...

You are due to go out for dinner with friends... You have been looking forward to this for weeks, but the day arrives and just a few hours before the meal, you start to feel like shit!
"What if I die on the way to the restaurant?"
"I'm going to be the ugliest one at the table."
"What if I get drunk and say something outrageous?"
"What if nobody on the table even actually likes me?"

Notice in this particular situation, the spiteful raisin has taken the form of an anxious, irrational thought......

<u>Clever, spiteful little man!</u>

Don't worry, help is at hand!

I want to break things down for a second to show you what I have come up with.
Hear me out...

Imagine for a second, we as human beings are broken up into 3 main parts:

The mind.

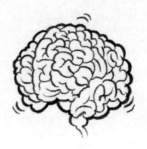

The mind is <u>GOOD!</u>
Your mind is on your side and
wants to be your friend.
In fact, it wants to be friends
with everyone and this can
sometimes be its downfall as it is
not that great at spotting
danger.

The body.

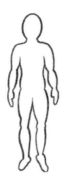

The body is also <u>GOOD!</u>
It also wants to be your friend.
Sometimes however,
unfortunately the body can
sometimes fall victim to bullying
from the spiteful raisin for
example feeling insecure, ugly
etc. but it is essentially just a
plastic carrier bag, carrying
around the mind and of course
the spiteful raisin.

The spiteful raisin.

The spiteful raisin is <u>BAD</u>!
In fact, the spiteful raisin is a
complete and utter prick!
This nasty little trouble maker is
a pest and will cause you trouble
every single day unless he is
dealt with accordingly.
He is a clever little man and can
change his disguise quickly and
efficiently.

The key to a peaceful mind is recognising when the spiteful raisin has started causing you trouble.
At first it will be difficult to spot this but over time you will become more familiar with his disguises and he will become easier to spot.

Most of the time, when you enter a fight with the spiteful raisin you won't even know it's happened.

This is usually the toughest part of the fight.

TASK:
Next time you find yourself
thinking anxious, irrational
thoughts or falling down the
rabbit hole of poor decision
making (drug abuse, self-harm
etc), try and stop your thoughts
just for a second, acknowledge
the fact that you have just
entered a fight with the spiteful
raisin and repeat after me. (you
can do this in your head.)

It's unlikely that the spiteful raisin will do as you say and just fuck off straight away, but that's ok don't worry.
He knows you have spotted him and now the next part is just as exciting.

See, the thing about the spiteful raisin and one of the main reasons he is so angry, is because he is small. Very small. And soft.

You are not small, or soft! You are much bigger and stronger than the spiteful raisin and because of this, you now get to decide how you want to deal with him.

Sometimes I like to just keep
telling him to fuck right off until
he does just that! This does
work, but can grow boring fairly
quickly.
So, use that overactive
imagination of yours and come
up with any fun, creative way
you choose to deal with the little
squirt.

**Hold the spiteful raisin
responsible for whatever
thought it is that's troubling
you** and punish him for it!

Squash him under your foot.
Throw him at a wall.
Bat him with a racket.

Whatever you decide to do, enjoy
it and take as much time as you
need to do it!

If you find yourself re-thinking the same thought again on repeat, don't worry! All this means is that the raisin has changed his disguise.
Well done for spotting it!
All you need to do is repeat the process.

Don't forget to remember the part where you hold him responsible for the thought. You must include this as part of your process every single time a troubling thought enters your head.
Even if it is the same thought as before!

Once you have done this, you can have fun and destroy him any way you choose!

This time however, maybe try a different, more creative way to get rid of the little pest.

You will usually find that even just discovering the spiteful raisin and allowing yourself to hold him responsible for the irrational thoughts will be enough to settle your mind and put the thought to rest.

It will give you a bit of breathing space and a time out from whatever it is that has been troubling you and as a result, you will find you have been a little bit kinder to yourself!

It's also a good idea to write yourself a list of reasons that you think may cause the spiteful raisin to show his ugly little face.

Here's a few of mine:

- Overtiredness
- Lack of exercise
- Too much coffee
- Too much time on social media
- Too much time watching tv.

Here is some space to write your own list:

1.

2.

3.

4.

5.

6.

7.

8.

9.

10.

Another great idea is to keep a record of occasions when you have entered a fight with the spiteful raisin and take note of how he disguised himself.
This will help you keep track of the thoughts that have troubled you and allow you to recognise how the spiteful raisin effected your mood before you spotted him and then destroyed him!

Keeping a record of his disguises means he will be easier to spot in the future.

There is plenty of space at the back of this book to do just that.

If you find that this simple technique just isn't quite enough, it's always a great idea to seek advice from a qualified professional.

Here is a list of some helpful charities/
phone numbers just in case you need them!

SAMARITANS: 116123

MIND: 0300 1233393

CALM: 0800 585858

SHOUT TEXT SERVICE: 85258

Lastly, be patient with yourself!
This technique may take a bit of
practice so don't be hard on
yourself if sometimes you don't
quite spot the raisin as quickly
as you would have liked.
He is the master of disguise after
all!

Good luck and don't forget to
share your stories on our
Instagram page!

@thespitefulraisin
#thespitefulraisin

Written by Glen Carloss

Don't forget to use this space to keep a record of the spiteful raisin...

Why were you fighting with the spiteful raisin and how did he disguise himself?

Did you hold him responsible for your thoughts?

How did you destroy him?

Give yourself a pat on the back!

Why were you fighting with the spiteful raisin and how did he disguise himself?

Did you hold him responsible for your thoughts?

How did you destroy him?

Give yourself a pat on the back!

Why were you fighting with the spiteful raisin and how did he disguise himself?

Did you hold him responsible for your thoughts?

How did you destroy him?

Give yourself a pat on the back!

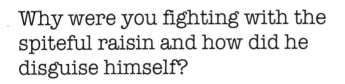

Why were you fighting with the spiteful raisin and how did he disguise himself?

Did you hold him responsible for your thoughts?

How did you destroy him?

Give yourself a pat on the back!

Why were you fighting with the spiteful raisin and how did he disguise himself?

Did you hold him responsible for your thoughts?

How did you destroy him?

Give yourself a pat on the back!

Why were you fighting with the spiteful raisin and how did he disguise himself?

Did you hold him responsible for your thoughts?

How did you destroy him?

Give yourself a pat on the back!